D0580221

SHADOW
Trapunto
GETA GRAMA
QUILTS

Simple Steps, Remarkable Results • 30 Elegant Projects

C&T PUBLISHING

Text and Artwork copyright © 2012 by Geta Grama

Photography and Artwork copyright © 2012 by C&T Publishing, Inc.

Publisher: Amy Marson

Creative Director: Gailen Runge

Acquisitions Editor: Susanne Woods

Editor: Liz Aneloski

Technical Editors: Sandy Peterson and Priscilla Read

Cover/Book Designer: April Mostek

Production Coordinator: Jessica Jenkins

Production Editor: Alice Mace Nakanishi

Illustrators: Geta Grama and Kirstie L. Pettersen

Photography by Dan Comaniciu, www.shots.ro, Brasov, Romania, unless otherwise noted

Published by C&T Publishing, Inc., P.O. Box 1456, Lafayette, CA 94549

Library of Congress Cataloging-in-Publication Data

Grama, Geta, 1968-

Shadow trapunto quilts : simple steps, remarkable results--30 elegant projects / Geta Grama.

  p. cm.

ISBN 978-1-60705-269-2 (soft cover)

1. Trapunto--Patterns. 2. Machine quilting--Patterns. I. Title.

TT835.G7225 2012

746.46--dc23

2011023294

Printed in China

10 9 8 7 6 5 4 3 2 1

Dedication

To my dear husband, Mircea.
This book is as much yours as it is mine.
I could never have followed the passion of my life
without your loving support.

Acknowledgments

Very special thanks go to the following individuals and companies:

My sister Oana

for introducing me to quilting

My sister Nina

for her invaluable help; she trimmed the batting away
for many projects in this book

My sister Nicoleta and my mother

for their constant encouragement and support

Michele Shatz (Florida)

for her involvement in this project, her advice, and her friendship

My Romanian and American quilting friends

for their support as I worked on the book,
especially for being creative in naming my quilts

Linda V. Taylor

for inspiring me to try shadow trapunto

Allie Heath and Robert Kaufman Fabrics

many of the quilts in this book are made with their wonderful fabrics

Penny McMorris and the Electric Quilt Company

for the best quilting software; all the designs in this book
were originally made using EQ6

Dana Jonsson and Valdani Inc.

many of my quilts are quilted with their beautiful variegated thread

Superior Threads

for manufacturing the wonderful Vanish-Extra water-soluble thread

C&T Publishing

for making it possible for me to share
my technique and my designs

Contents

My Journey to Shadow Trapunto

From time to time I feel sorry that I live in Romania, a country where the word *quilt* is unknown to most people. I can't find the essential materials I need for quilting (such as fabrics and batting), and I don't have very many friends to share my passion with. But then I realize that these challenges have helped me grow as a quilter and led me to write this book.

All I know about quilting I have learned on my own from books, from the Internet, and from my mistakes. During my first two years of quilting, I made quilts, but I was not sure whether they were really quilts or not because I hadn't ever seen a real quilt. At the time, I did not have anyone to get advice from, so I was forced to do things as best I could and in my own way.

A few years ago I saw Linda V. Taylor in a show on the Internet making a colored shadow trapunto quilt. Seduced by the technique she used, I tried to make a shadow trapunto quilt myself. Unable to find the cotton batiste she used, I adapted the technique to what I could find here in Romania. And so I started making quilts using the technique presented in this book.

My passion for shadow trapunto grew when I started to combine this technique with the designs I made using the Electric Quilt Company software EQ. I have an engineering background, and I love to use the computer to draw my designs. I am a big fan of this software, as it makes my technique easier to implement.

About This Book

The Getting Started chapter (page 8) will introduce you to the supplies you need to make shadow trapunto quilts. In the following chapters, the shadow trapunto technique is explained in detail. Then you can take the technique further and add new dimension to your quilts by combining shadow trapunto with other quilting techniques. If you don't have very much time for quilting, you can make postcards—you can learn how to make them using my *Daisy Postcard* pattern (page 44), or you can use your own designs.

A major part of the book is devoted to instructions for 30 projects. Experiment with the designs as they are or use them as inspiration to create your own designs. I have also included the Gallery (page 58) of my other shadow trapunto work.

I hope the ideas and techniques presented in this book will inspire you to start creating your own shadow trapunto quilts—you may be opening a new chapter in your quilting life! Enjoy!

Shadow Trapunto Technique at a Glance

My finished quilts have five layers to them. From top to bottom, the layers are organza, trapunto motifs made from batting, background fabric, batting, and backing. The white design of the quilt top is made from the organza and trapunto motifs that are placed on the familiar "quilt sandwich" made from the background fabric, batting, and backing.

Over the last three years I have received many questions from quilters wondering how I make my quilts. How is the white design created? Are the designs painted? Where does the glow come from? Here is a brief explanation of the technique:

1. Print the pattern design on paper. Place the organza on a layer of thick batting and the paper pattern design on top of the organza. *Pin through all the layers.*

Front

Back

2. Using your sewing machine, stitch on the design lines through the paper, organza, and batting with water-soluble thread.

3. Remove the paper.

4. Trim away the batting from around the design motifs.

Note: Do not trim away the organza.

5. Layer the trimmed organza/batting piece on top of the quilt front, batting, and backing fabric (the quilt sandwich).

6. Stitch around the design motifs, quilt the background space around the trapunto design, and bind.

As you can see, batting—the layer of a quilt that is never visible—is the star of my quilts.

You need only a few simple supplies to make shadow trapunto quilts.

The Patterns

You have two options for creating the patterns on paper. You can photocopy or scan and print the patterns in the book using the enlargement percentages given in the project instructions, or you can print them from the enclosed CD.

The patterns for all the projects are provided on the enclosed CD as PDF files. Most patterns are printed on multiple pages. All you have to do is tape them together. To easily tape one page to another, remove the right margin of the first page by cutting on the dashed line and tape the first page to the second page, and so on across the row. Remove any excess margin paper from

the back of the taped pattern. Use a similar method to tape the rows together.

Remove right margin of first page and tape first page to second page, and continue until you have taped all pages and all rows together. Remove any excess margin paper from back of taped pattern.

Photo by C&T Publishing

Notes

- I recommend that you print the patterns from the files on the enclosed CD rather than enlarging and printing them from the book, because the line weights will remain thin so there will be less chance of ink transfer to the organza.

- Use Adobe Reader (a free download from www.adobe.com) to open and print the PDF files.

Paper for Printing the Patterns

Use paper that is thinner than the paper you normally use with your printer; newsprint paper or 60g/m²-weight paper or a little heavier will work fine. I usually use Carol Doak's Foundation Paper (by C&T Publishing). It is easy to stitch through and tears away easily when the stitching is finished. Always make sure you are printing the patterns on the proper paper. If you are not sure about a paper, try printing and stitching with a small pattern first to test.

Options

You can also use the patterns as appliqué, trapunto, stenciling, or quilting designs.

Front of Doily Delight

Back of Doily Delight. This gives you an idea of what design would look like as wholecloth, trapunto, or quilting design.

Organza

There are many types of organza on the market. I use 100% nylon sparkling white or ivory organza that is 58″ wide. For shadow trapunto, the best organza has a stiff, rough, crisp feel and is as sheer as possible. It is stable and keeps its shape very well. This type of organza is used in dressmaking and is different from the type used for curtains. It is also used in gift packaging. Organza can be found in different widths.

For small projects, any type of organza works. For projects larger than 30″, avoid using a soft, silky, and slippery organza. It is easier to work with stable fabric.

Any sheer fabric (such as batiste or voile) that allows the color of the layer behind it to show through can also be used.

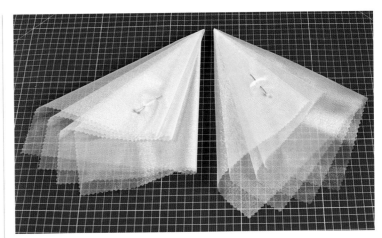

Stiff organza

Iron organza carefully. Do not use a hot iron but do use steam. Don't worry if some creases remain after ironing; they will not show up in the finished quilt.

Trapunto Batting

I use thick, fluffy, airy polyester batting in all my shadow trapunto projects—weighted at 3.5–6 ounces per square yard (120–200g/m²) with a loft of approximately ½″. Hobbs Poly-Down Plus batting is not too thick and trims away easily. Poly-fil Hi-Loft batting (by Fairfield) is thicker and the cutting process takes a little more time, but this product has the advantage of creating a high contrast with the background fabric. I like this type of fluffy, airy batting because it can be easily cut away and the stitched motifs look wonderful under the organza. The design looks like it is drawn in the snow.

How the batting is bonded affects how well it will work. If the batting tears easily, you can cut it away easily, too. A dense, compact batting with fibers that hold together very well and with a smooth, solid surface is harder to cut away, even when it is fluffy.

Fluffy, airy batting that tears easily

- Do not use a trapunto batting that is too thin—the color of the background fabric underneath the trapunto motif might show through. But do not use a batting that is too thick and dense, either—it will be difficult to cut it away, especially if you have an intricate design, and it will also be a challenge to lay the uneven trimmed organza/batting piece flat against the background fabric. You want the batting to be thick enough for good contrast and to prevent show-through but thin enough to be trimmed easily.

- For small projects or complex designs, use a slightly thinner batting than you would use with larger projects or simple designs.

- Do not use feltlike batting, even if it is polyester. The look of the quilt will not be the same, and, more important, the batting will be difficult to cut away.

- Two layers of very thin batting can be used instead of a thick batting if the weight does not exceed 5–6 ounces per square yard (170–200g/m²). Cutting away excess batting should not be a problem, but cutting through two layers is more difficult than cutting through only one layer.

Sewing a Sample

I recommend that you sew small samples using different battings with your organza to see if you like the look of the batting under the organza and to test how easy it is to cut away the batting.

Enlarge and print the Batting Test pattern (page 69) or print the paper pattern using the file on the CD (battingtest.pdf). This pattern prints out at 6″ × 6″. Prepare the layers of the paper design, organza, and batting and stitch around the motifs with water-soluble thread. Practice cutting away the batting, make the quilt sandwich, and then finish stitch around the motifs with your thread of choice. Next, practice quilting through the quilt sandwich and decide which types of batting work the best for you.

Quilt Batting

Use the batting you normally use in your quilts for the middle layer of the quilt sandwich. For most of the quilts in this book, I used the same fluffy polyester batting I used for the trapunto motifs;

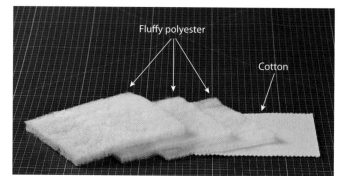

Batting for trapunto and middle layer of quilt sandwich

it creates nice definition in the quilting. However, the quilting was much easier on the quilts made using a flat cotton batting. Now I use cotton batting for quilts larger than 25″ square.

Background Fabric

This is the fabric under the trimmed organza/batting piece. It also forms the top layer of the usual quilt sandwich. Use cotton quilting fabric in bold, bright colors that will enhance and contrast with the trapunto design; see Tips for Choosing Background Fabric (page 15).

Backing Fabric

Use the fabric you usually use for backing your quilts. For most of my quilts, I use white cotton because the white of the fabric allows the stitched trapunto design to show up clearly on the back of the quilt.

Notes

Prewashing

- Prewash all cotton fabrics used for the background or backing.

- If the batting used in the middle layer of the quilt sandwich might shrink (per package instructions), prewash it.

- Do not prewash the organza; you want it to remain stiff.

- Do not prewash the polyester trapunto batting because it won't shrink.

Water-Soluble Thread

The trapunto design is stitched first using water-soluble thread. I use Vanish-Extra thread (by Superior Threads). You can use this thread as the top thread and thin white thread in the bobbin, but I always use water-soluble thread in both the top and the bobbin. That way, I don't have to worry about thread tension problems or the bobbin thread showing in the design after washing the water-soluble thread away.

Water-soluble thread is expensive in small spools, so I usually buy it in 1,500-yard spools. It can be found in spools of 200 yards; one spool will be enough if you want to stitch just one medium-size design (20"–25" square) from this book. This thread can also be used for basting a quilt.

Note

For miniatures, working with water-soluble thread in the bobbin is a must. Because the motifs are very small and the batting is relatively thin, a bobbin thread that does not wash out might show on the final quilt.

Scissors for Trimming Trapunto Batting

Thread snips (thread clippers) are the magical tool I use to cut the batting away. They can be used for hours without hand pain or creating blisters on fingers. They fit comfortably in the hand and spring open after each snip. The snips measure about 4¼" long. The small size and the short blades allow better control while trimming, which means less chance of accidentally snipping the organza.

Thread snips

These snips, along with the correct batting for trapunto (page 10), make a great team for easy trimming. Trimming a flat, dense batting is not as easy.

Notes

- I always keep thread snips at hand while I am sewing. They are the best tool for snipping thread while piecing or cleaning up the edges of the quilt before adding binding.

- There are versions of these thread snips that have a ring on one of the handles. They are perfect for clipping thread but are not as comfortable for cutting the batting away.

Thread for Finish Stitching Motifs and Quilting

I usually finish stitch the trapunto motifs (the second row of stitching around the motifs) with white thread, using a weight that fits the look I want. For quilting the background around the design motifs, I use #40/3 quilting thread, and if I want more defined quilting I use a thicker thread (#30/3).

For more information about quilting thread, see Machine Stitching, Quilting, and Finishing (page 16).

Machine Needles

Schmetz Topstitch #14/90 needles are the only needles I use for making a quilt from start to finish. They have large eyes and prevent shredding and thread breaks. I keep a needle only for stitching through paper, and I have another needle for finish stitching around the motifs and for quilting the background.

Sewing Machine

Be sure your machine is clean and oiled. For free-motion stitching, use a darning (free-motion quilting) foot and lower the feed dogs. If you can't lower the feed dogs, cover them with a piece of plastic. *When stitching through the paper pattern, use small stitches (2mm) so the paper tears away easily and doesn't distort the stitches.*

Shadow Trapunto Tutorial— Foliage

The following instructions will walk you through the process of shadow trapunto step by step.

ORGANZA: 19″ × 19½″ (Cut each dimension at least 3″ larger than the finished size of the project.)

TRAPUNTO BATTING: 19″ × 19½″ (Cut the same size as the organza.)

BACKGROUND FABRIC: 21″ × 21½″ (Cut each dimension at least 5″ larger than the finished size of the project.)

FLAT BATTING: 21″ × 21½″ (Cut the same size as the background fabric.)

BACKING FABRIC: 21″ × 21½″ (Cut the same size as the background fabric.)

BINDING: 1 pieced strip 2½″ × 75″

Foliage, approximately 16″ × 16½″

Print the Pattern

Enlarge and print the *Foliage* Tutorial pattern (page 69) or print and assemble the paper pattern using the file on the CD (foliagetutorial.pdf).

Pattern size: 15″ × 15″

Stitch the Trapunto Design

1. Layer the batting (on the bottom), organza (in the middle), and the paper pattern (on top), centering the pattern on the organza.

2. Use straight pins to pin the 3 layers together. Position the points of the pins in the middle layer of the sandwich to avoid pricking yourself.

3. Using water-soluble thread, stitch on the paper design lines with small stitches. When stitching through the paper pattern, use small stitches (2mm) so the paper tears away easily and doesn't distort the stitches. I use water-soluble thread not only in the needle but in the bobbin, too. Stitch from the outside of the pattern to the center. For larger quilts, after you stitch the outside area, remove the already-stitched

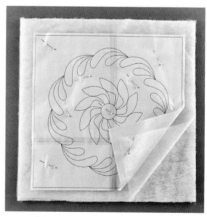

Layered batting, organza, and paper pattern

paper for easier access to the center. (*Be careful* not to tear the unsewn paper.) *Remember:* Use the needle designated for stitching through paper in this step.

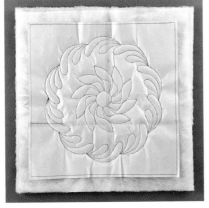

Stitches on front

Stitches on back

4. After the entire pattern is stitched, remove the remaining paper. The tiny pieces of paper left in the stitches can be removed using the tip of your thread snips or tweezers.

Cut Away the Trapunto Batting

Method 1: Between Close Motifs or Inside Motifs

With the batting layer on top and the organza on the bottom, place your left hand under the organza while keeping your left thumb over the top of the batting in the area where you want to cut (right hand and thumb for left-handers). Keep the organza flat while you move the tips of the snips to cut away the batting in this small area.

Method 1

Method 2: Around and Outside Motifs

Lay the project on a flat surface, with the organza on the bottom and the batting on top, and keep both hands on top of the batting. Gently peel back the batting as the snips cut the batting away.

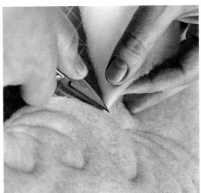

Method 2

Use Method 1 for cutting batting away inside motif and Method 2 for cutting batting away around motif.

From the batting side and working from the center out, carefully cut away the batting between and around the motifs using either Method 1 or Method 2 (above). To make the first cut in an area, insert the tip of the snips into the batting and carefully make a small cut without clipping the organza. Trim the batting as close to the stitching as possible without snipping the bobbin thread. Keep the organza flat while you are trimming to avoid making holes in the organza with the tip of the thread snips.

Center section cut away, viewed from back side

Batting cut away, viewed from back side

Choose the Background Fabric

The background fabric functions as the top layer of the quilt sandwich as well as being the background for the trimmed organza/batting piece. Test a few fabrics. Lay the organza/batting piece over each fabric and see which one looks best. Keep in mind that after the final quilting the color of the fabric will look more intense.

Audition background fabrics

Printing the Pattern

- The given pattern size is the size of the bounding square surrounding the design motifs. The height and width of the actual trapunto design motifs may be smaller than the pattern size, depending on the pattern you are using.

- Don't try to take a shortcut and transfer the pattern onto the organza. You need the paper as a heavy stabilizer when stitching through both the organza and the batting.

Using Pins Versus Adhesive

Do not use temporary adhesive instead of pins. (You want the batting to remain free so that you can cut it away.)

TIPS

Working with Water-Soluble Thread

- Keep the spool of water-soluble thread away from water.

- Be careful not to confuse a bobbin of water-soluble thread with one holding normal thread (or vice versa).

- I don't put the large spool of water-soluble thread on the sewing machine; I use a metal cone holder placed near the sewing machine because of the large spool size.

Machine Stitching

- Lower the tension of the top thread if necessary.

- Start and stop stitching with 3–4 dense backstitches.

- Do not cut the threads after you finish an area and want to move to a close area to continue stitching. Just lift the darning foot, move the next area under the needle, lower the darning foot, and start the new stitching.

- Sew with an evenly balanced stitch, but don't keep readjusting the tension of the threads if you can't get the perfect stitch. *Remember:* Those stitches will disappear after you wash the quilt.

- For stitching straight-line designs (see Stitch the Trapunto Design, Step 3, page 12), I use a walking foot.

Working with Batting

If there are places where the trapunto batting pulls away from the stitching, thread a needle with water-soluble thread and baste that section of the batting in place.

Choosing Background Fabric

- Do not use light-colored fabric (there will not be enough contrast between the batting motifs and the fabric, and the design will not show up well).

- Bold and bright colors work well to produce a high contrast with the white batting motifs.

- A narrow design can be accentuated by bold colors and blended by light colors.

- If you want to use multicolor fabrics, choose fabrics with colors of similar value. Fabrics that contain both light and dark will not allow your design to look its best.

- Striped fabric and geometric prints work wonderfully.

- Solid-colored fabrics emphasize a design.

Layering the Sandwich

1. Stretch the backing fabric (wrong side up) on a table, using masking tape or paper clamps (also called binder clips); then layer the flat batting, the background fabric (right side up), and the trimmed organza/batting piece (centered on the background fabric with the organza side up). Follow this step regardless of the size of the quilt. This prevents creases on the back of the quilt.

2. Beginning at the center, pin the layers in place with straight pins (or safety pins if you prefer). Position the points of the straight pins in the middle layer.

TIP Smooth Trapunto Design

No matter how bonded the batting is, sometimes small pieces of batting migrate onto the background fabric outside the trapunto motifs, under the organza. If this occurs, pull them back into position under the organza with the tip of a pin.

Finish Stitching around the Trapunto Design

Stitch around the trapunto motifs following the edge of the batting rather than the stitching made with water-soluble thread; if you didn't cut away the batting close enough to the water-soluble stitching, it won't be noticeable. Do not stitch over the batting; keep it inside the stitching lines.

I usually use white thread as the top thread in my sewing machine. If the design requires much backtracking (stitching back on top of previous stitches), I would recommend that you use a fine thread so you don't accentuate those stitches. A few of my quilts are quilted with invisible thread.

In the bobbin, I almost always use white thread because I prefer to use the same color of thread in both the needle and the bobbin. If I can match the backing with the bobbin thread, that's even better.

Sometimes I prefer to outline the trapunto with a contrasting color of thread. I match its color with the color of the background fabric.

TIPS Machine Stitching

- If you need to backtrack, take your time and stitch exactly over the previous stitches. It's worth the effort.

- Stitch the straight lines using a walking foot.

- Start and stop the stitches with a few small backstitches.

Continuous-Line Finish Stitching

Many of the trapunto motifs in this book can be stitched from start to finish in one continuous line of stitching, even when they look like they require two lines of stitching. For the design below, I first stitch the entire inside part (following the red arrows), stopping and turning at the red intersection points. Then I stitch the outside part (following the blue arrows). The entire design is completed in one continuous line of stitching.

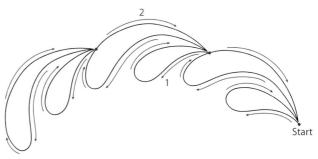

One continuous line of stitching: red line first, then blue line

Quilting the Background

The background is quilted around and between the trapunto motifs. Dense quilting makes the trapunto design stand out even more. Fancy quilting would look nice, but a simple, dense stippling pattern works just fine.

I always quilt from the center out to the edges in a circular path.

Stitching in a Circular Path

For designs with separate inner and outer wreaths such as the *Foliage* design (see photo below), I finish stitch the trapunto design and quilt the background all at once. This reduces the likelihood of puckers forming. First, stitch the center wreath (1) and then stitch the background between this wreath and the outer wreath (2). Next, finish stitch the outer wreath (3), and finally quilt the background outside the outer wreath (4).

Quilting in circular path

TIPS Machine Quilting

- If you need to stitch circles, take your time because any mistakes will be noticeable.

- Areas of very dense quilting in white thread give a shaded appearance.

Note

Free-Motion Quilting

Most of the designs in this book require free-motion stitching. Don't be intimidated if you are a beginner quilter; this technique will allow you to improve your skills. Free-motion quilting is something that anyone can do. It just takes *practice!*

I can honestly say that I was a bit scared when I stitched for the first time using the free-motion technique. After the first stitches I was sure that I would never be able to do it. But after a little practice I felt comfortable moving the quilt freely under the needle, and I became more confident.

Of course, I also thought stitching a design following a pattern drawn on paper would be extremely hard and only the experts could do it. But I was wrong again. It is really easy. You don't have to struggle to see the pattern lines on paper because they are clearly visible. Your only concern is to follow them. Run your machine slowly and don't look at the needle; look at the next small portion of the line you will be stitching.

Many patterns in this book can be used for practicing free-motion quilting. Print what you want on paper and pin the paper on a small quilt sandwich. You can practice stitching the pattern even without threading the needle. Soon you will realize that free-motion quilting is a lot of fun.

The original design may shrink a little after all the stitching is complete. You may experience shrinkage of up to an inch or so for small quilts and even more for larger quilts.

Washing the Quilt

After all the background quilting is finished, wash the quilt to remove the chemicals and water-soluble thread. Immerse it in medium-temperature water for a few minutes, using a light detergent. If there are any ink marks on the organza, gently rub the spots using a soft toothbrush and some detergent.

Rinse out the quilt and put it in the washing machine for a short cycle of spinning (2–3 minutes, 300–400 rotations per minute). Use a gentle spin cycle so you don't remove all the water. Take the quilt out of the washing machine and smooth it out on a flat surface to dry. An iron is not needed to smooth the quilt.

I do all these steps no matter whether I make a postcard or a large quilt.

The design motifs look great after washing. There is a single row of stitches around the batting motifs. *Note that additional shrinkage may occur during washing.*

Quilt after washing

Squaring Up the Quilt

It's time to give your quilt its final shape. It is easy to trim it square or rectangular.

1. Place a square ruler over the quilt, in the upper right corner. For a square quilt with a circular design, the edges of the ruler must be placed at the same distance from the outer edge of the design on all 4 sides in order to keep the design in the center of the quilt. For *Foliage* (page 12), I placed the edges of the ruler 2″ away from the outermost points of the design on the top and right side of the quilt.

2. Cut along the ruler edges. If the quilt is bigger than the square ruler, use a long ruler to finish the cut. Then rotate the quilt, place the ruler on the next corner in the same way, and cut. Repeat for all the corners.

Squaring up quilt

> ### Note
> **Final Size of Quilt**
> The distances to trim from the edges of the stitched design motifs are given in the project directions. Note that the design motif dimensions may be smaller than the given pattern size, depending on the pattern you are using. (*Remember:* The pattern size is the overall size of the square box around the design motifs.) The given project size is approximate due to variable shrinkage when you stitch. You can adjust the final size of the quilt to your own needs by simply making it a little smaller or larger as you square up the quilt.

Quilts with More than Four Sides

Some of my designs are square and others are circular (wreaths). All are made out of quadrants or wedges that are repeated a number of times. If you don't want a square quilt, you can make it into a shape with the number of edges equal to the number of wedge repeats. As examples, a design with 8 equal wedge-shaped repeats can be cut as an octagon, and a design with 6 equal wedge-shaped repeats can be cut as a hexagon. *Fortune Wheel* (page 25) has 12 repeats and 12 sides.

Follow these steps to cut a quilt into the shape you want.

1. Choose the outermost 2 points of a wedge design repeat (points A and B).

2. Place a ruler over the quilt, with the edge of the ruler at the desired distance from the 2 selected points. Draw a line along the edge of the ruler, using a water-soluble pencil.

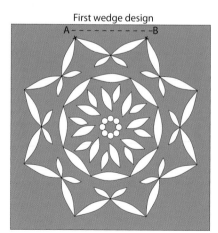
Choose 2 points and mark.

Second wedge design

First wedge design

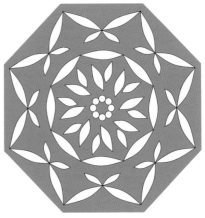

Choose next 2 points and mark.

All points marked

Perfect octagonal shape

3. Rotate the quilt counterclockwise. Choose the same 2 points of the second wedge design and repeat Step 2. (Here, point B of the first wedge design is also point A in the second wedge design, but this might not be true for all designs.)

4. Repeat all the way around the quilt. All the sides of the shape should have the same length. Make adjustments if necessary.

5. Cut along the drawn lines using a ruler and a rotary cutter.

Now the quilt is ready for binding!

Finishing

If you want more color on your quilts, you can finish them with piping, ruffles, or prairie points, using fabrics that are different from the background. For some ideas, look at *Cranberry Pie* (page 48), *Edelweiss* (page 43), and *Raindrops on the Lake* (page 36).

Double-Fold Binding

After you give your quilt a perfect shape, here is how to stitch a perfect binding that finishes to ⅜″ wide.

Follow these directions for binding quilts with 4 or more sides.

1. Cut 2½″-wide strips. Piece the strips to a length 10″ longer than the perimeter of the quilt. Fold the joined strip in half lengthwise, wrong sides together, and press.

2. Start the binding along the first edge. Line up the raw edges of the binding with the edge of the quilt, right sides together. Mark half the angle between the first and second adjacent edges with a pin near the outer edge of the quilt.

10-sided quilt

3. Start stitching a few inches from the end of the binding using a ¼″ seam allowance. Stop and backstitch when you reach the pin. Remove the quilt from the sewing machine.

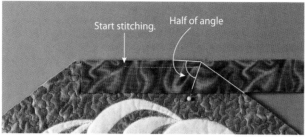

Mark half of angle with pin and stitch.

4. Flip the binding up so it is parallel with the second edge of the quilt and the fold divides the corner angle in half. Be sure to keep the binding in line with this second edge to be sewn. Pin to keep the fold in place.

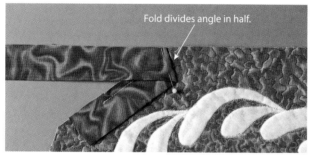

Flip binding and pin.

5. Fold the binding back down so its raw edge is aligned with the second edge to be sewn. Pin. As in Step 2, mark half the angle between this edge and the third adjacent edge with a pin. Stitch along the second edge. Stop and backstitch when you reach the pin. Remove the quilt from the sewing machine.

Fold binding down and stitch.

6. Repeat Steps 4 and 5 sequentially for all the edges of the quilt. Join the binding ends using your favorite method.

7. Fold the binding to the back of the quilt and stitch it down. I pin the binding by inserting the pins on the front of the quilt, keeping the pins parallel with the fold of the binding. Then I stitch in-the-ditch along the binding, catching the binding edge on the back of the quilt at the same time.

Front   *Back*

Making a Pillow

After a quilted pillow top is finished, I like to make it into a removable pillow cover so it can be washed.

Making a Pillow Form

If you can't find a ready-made pillow form (because of the shape or size of your pillow), you'll have to make one. Make it the same size and shape as the pillow top.

1. Cut 2 pieces of muslin the size of the pillow top. Place them right sides together and, using ½″ seam allowances, sew around the edge, leaving an opening for turning.

2. Turn the piece right side out and stuff it with loose polyester fiberfill to the desired firmness.

3. Stitch the opening closed by hand or by machine.

> ## Note
> **Correct Size of Pillow Form**
> If your pillow has a flange, make the pillow insert after the pillow cover is finished, since the interior size will be smaller than the original pillow top size.

Making the Pillow Back

1. Measure the quilted pillow top (the front of the pillow).

2. From the fabric you want to use for the pillow back, cut a piece 2″ wider and 8″ longer than the measurements from Step 1.

3. Cut this piece in half, parallel to the shorter sides.

4. Hem the 2 edges you just cut (fold the raw edges under ½″, fold them under again, and stitch using matching thread).

5. Overlap the hemmed sides 4″.

6. Secure the 2 pieces together by stitching a few inches at each end (see the yellow marking). The length of the stitched section depends on the size of the pillow; leave an opening large enough to easily insert the pillow form.

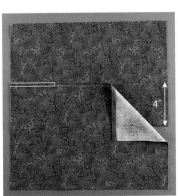

Prepare pillow back.

Strengthen the vertical seam by backstitching.

Pillow Closure

Cut a 3″ piece of hook-and-loop tape, separate the 2 pieces, and center and stitch a piece to each side of the pillow opening.

Add hook-and-loop tape.

Finishing the Pillow

Attach the quilted front to the back in either of two ways:

Option 1

This method will leave exposed the raw edges, which will need to be covered with traditional quilt binding.

1. Place the front and back with the wrong sides together, centering the front on the back, and pin.

2. Stitch around the front edges with ⅛″ seam allowances. Trim the back even with the front.

Stitch with wrong sides together.

3. Add binding covering the ⅛″ seam allowances.

Option 2

1. Place the front and back with the right sides together, centering the front on the back, and pin.

2. Stitch around the front edges with ½″ seam allowances. Trim the back even with the front.

Stitch with right sides together.

3. Finish the edges with a dense zigzag (or satin) stitch. Then turn the pillow cover right side out.

Creating a Flange

1. After completing the steps for Option 2, determine how wide you want the flange around the perimeter of the pillow. This is where you will add a second line of stitching on all 4 sides of the pillow. For instance, if you want a flange width of 3″, measure 3″ in from the edges of the pillow on all sides; add stitching. If you want to use a ready-made pillow form, measure the distance inside the proposed stitching lines to be sure you can find a pillow form to fit. Note that you need to plan ahead for this when sizing the opening on the back side of the pillow.

2. Stitch all the way around the sides, through all the layers, using the distance from the edge determined in Step 1.

Waves

QUILT SIZE: approximately 26½″ × 26½″ | **PATTERN SIZE:** 25″ × 25″

Materials and Cutting

ORGANZA: 29½″ × 29½″

TRAPUNTO BATTING: 29½″ × 29½″

BACKGROUND FABRIC: 31½″ × 31½″

QUILT BATTING: 31½″ × 31½″

BACKING FABRIC: 31½″ × 31½″

BINDING: 1 pieced strip 2½″ × 116″

Instructions

Enlarge and print the *Waves* pattern (page 70) or print and assemble the paper pattern using the file on the CD (waves.pdf). For pattern instructions, refer to The Patterns (page 8).

Create the trapunto design and then machine stitch, quilt, and finish the piece. Refer to Shadow Trapunto Technique at a Glance (page 6); Getting Started (page 8);

Shadow Trapunto Tutorial (page 12); and Machine Stitching, Quilting, and Finishing (page 16) for general information.

After washing the piece, trim the edges ¾″ from the outermost points of the design on all 4 sides and bind.

Indian Summer

PILLOW SIZE: approximately 19″ × 19″ (including flange) | **PATTERN SIZE:** 20″ × 20″

Materials and Cutting

ORGANZA: 23″ × 23″

TRAPUNTO BATTING: 23″ × 23″

BACKGROUND FABRIC: 25″ × 25″

QUILT BATTING: 25″ × 25″

BACKING FABRIC: 25″ × 25″

PILLOW BACK FABRIC: 2 pieces 22″ × 14″

SQUARE PILLOW FORM: 16″ × 16″

Instructions

Enlarge and print the *Indian Summer* pattern (page 71) or print and assemble the paper pattern using the file on the CD (indiansummer.pdf). For pattern instructions, refer to The Patterns (page 8).

Create the trapunto design and then machine stitch, quilt, and finish the piece. Refer to Shadow Trapunto Technique at a Glance (page 6); Getting Started (page 8); Shadow Trapunto Tutorial (page 12); and Machine Stitching, Quilting, and Finishing (page 16) for general information.

After washing the quilt top, trim the edges of the piece ¾″ away from the outermost points of the diamond border.

Hem a long side on each of the 2 pillow back pieces, assemble the pillow back, and add a hook-and-loop tape closure (see Making the Pillow Back, page 21).

Attach the pillow front to the back, right sides together, using a ½″ seam allowance. Turn the pillow cover right side out. To form the flange, topstitch through all the layers about ¼″ inside the diamond border so that the diamond border is centered on the flange. Insert the pillow form.

Round Dance of Christmas Trees

QUILT SIZE: approximately 14″ × 12″ | **PATTERN SIZE:** 12″ × 12″

Materials and Cutting

ORGANZA: 17″ × 15″

TRAPUNTO BATTING: 17″ × 15″

BACKGROUND FABRIC: 19″ × 17″

QUILT BATTING: 19″ × 17″

BACKING FABRIC: 19″ × 17″

BINDING: 1 pieced strip 2½″ × 55″

Instructions

Enlarge and print the *Round Dance of Christmas Trees* pattern (page 71) or print and assemble the paper pattern using the file on the CD (rounddanceofchristmastrees.pdf). For pattern instructions, refer to The Patterns (page 8).

Create the trapunto design and then machine stitch, quilt, and finish the piece. Refer to Shadow Trapunto Technique at a Glance (page 6); Getting Started (page 8); Shadow Trapunto Tutorial (page 12); and Machine Stitching, Quilting, and Finishing (page 16) for general information.

After washing the piece, trim the edges 1″ from the outermost points of the design (see Quilts with More than Four Sides, page 18) and bind.

Fortune Wheel

QUILT SIZE: approximately 18″ × 18″ | **PATTERN SIZE:** 16″ × 16″

Materials and Cutting

ORGANZA: 21″ × 21″

TRAPUNTO BATTING: 21″ × 21″

BACKGROUND FABRIC: 23″ × 23″

QUILT BATTING: 23″ × 23″

BACKING FABRIC: 23″ × 23″

BINDING: 1 pieced strip 2½″ × 70″

Instructions

Enlarge and print the *Fortune Wheel* pattern (page 71) or print and assemble the paper pattern using the file on the CD (fortunewheel.pdf). For pattern instructions, refer to The Patterns (page 8).

Create the trapunto design and then machine stitch, quilt, and finish the piece. Refer to Shadow Trapunto Technique at a Glance (page 6); Getting Started (page 8); Shadow Trapunto Tutorial (page 12); and Machine Stitching, Quilting, and Finishing (page 16) for general information.

After washing the piece, trim the edges 1½″ from the outermost points of the design (see Quilts with More than Four Sides, page 18) and bind.

A New Beginning

QUILT SIZE: approximately 17″ × 17″ | **PATTERN SIZE:** 15″ × 15″

Materials and Cutting

ORGANZA: 20″ × 20″

TRAPUNTO BATTING: 20″ × 20″

BACKGROUND FABRIC: 22″ × 22″

QUILT BATTING: 22″ × 22″

BACKING FABRIC: 22″ × 22″

BINDING: 1 pieced strip 2½″ × 78″

Instructions

Enlarge and print the *A New Beginning* pattern (page 69) or print and assemble the paper pattern using the file on the CD (anewbeginning.pdf). For pattern instructions, refer to The Patterns (page 8).

Create the trapunto design and then machine stitch, quilt, and finish the piece. Refer to Shadow Trapunto Technique at a Glance (page 6); Getting Started (page 8); Shadow Trapunto Tutorial (page 12); and Machine Stitching, Quilting, and Finishing (page 16) for general information. Note the effect of the striped fabric I used for the background.

After washing the piece, trim the edges 1½″ from the outermost points of the design and bind.

Waiting for Spring

QUILT SIZE: approximately 18″ × 41″ | **PATTERN SIZE:** 20″ × 40″

Materials and Cutting

ORGANZA: 21″ × 44″

TRAPUNTO BATTING: 21″ × 44″

BACKGROUND FABRIC: 23″ × 46″

QUILT BATTING: 23″ × 46″

BACKING FABRIC: 23″ × 46″

BINDING: 1 pieced strip 2½″ × 128″

Instructions

Enlarge and print the *Waiting for Spring* pattern (page 72) or print and assemble the paper pattern using the file on the CD (waitingforspring.pdf). For pattern instructions, refer to The Patterns (page 8).

Create the trapunto design and then machine stitch, quilt, and finish the piece. Refer to Shadow Trapunto Technique at a Glance (page 6); Getting Started (page 8); Shadow Trapunto Tutorial (page 12); and Machine Stitching, Quilting, and Finishing (page 16) for general information.

After washing the piece, trim the edges 1″ from the outermost edge of the border and bind.

Lights into the Dark

QUILT SIZE: approximately 16″ × 39″ | **PATTERN SIZE:** 16½″ × 38″

Materials and Cutting

ORGANZA: 19″ × 42″

TRAPUNTO BATTING: 19″ × 42″

BACKGROUND FABRIC: 21″ × 44″

QUILT BATTING: 21″ × 44″

BACKING FABRIC: 21″ × 44″

BINDING: 1 pieced strip 2½″ × 120″

Instructions

Enlarge and print the *Lights into the Dark* pattern (page 73) or print and assemble the paper pattern using the file on the CD (lightsintothedark.pdf). For pattern instructions, refer to The Patterns (page 8).

Create the trapunto design and then machine stitch, quilt, and finish the piece. Refer to Shadow Trapunto Technique at a Glance (page 6); Getting Started (page 8); Shadow Trapunto Tutorial (page 12); and Machine Stitching, Quilting, and Finishing (page 16) for general information.

After washing the piece, trim the edges ¾″ from the outermost points of the border and bind.

Polar Night

QUILT SIZE: approximately 25″ × 22″ | **PATTERN SIZE:** 20″ × 20″

Materials and Cutting

ORGANZA: 28″ × 25″

TRAPUNTO BATTING: 28″ × 25″

BACKGROUND FABRIC: 30″ × 27″

QUILT BATTING: 30″ × 27″

BACKING FABRIC: 30″ × 27″

BINDING: 1 pieced strip 2½″ × 85″

Instructions

Enlarge and print the *Polar Night* pattern (page 75) or print and assemble the paper pattern using the file on the CD (polarnight.pdf). For pattern instructions, refer to The Patterns (page 8).

Create the trapunto design and then machine stitch, quilt, and finish the piece. Refer to Shadow Trapunto Technique at a Glance (page 6); Getting Started (page 8); Shadow Trapunto Tutorial (page 12); and Machine Stitching, Quilting, and Finishing (page 16) for general information.

After washing the piece, trim the edges 2″ from the outermost points of the star's border (see Quilts with More than Four Sides, page 18) and bind.

Lacy Flower

QUILT SIZE: 12½″ diameter | **PATTERN SIZE:** 8″ × 8″

Materials and Cutting

ORGANZA: 16″ × 16″

TRAPUNTO BATTING: 16″ × 16″

BACKGROUND FABRIC: 18″ × 18″

QUILT BATTING: 18″ × 18″

BACKING FABRIC: 18″ × 18″

BINDING: 1 pieced bias strip 2½″ × 50″

TRANSPARENT PLASTIC TEMPLATE:
12½″ diameter

PERMANENT MARKER

Instructions

Enlarge and print the *Lacy Flower* pattern (page 69) or print and assemble the paper pattern using the file on the CD (lacyflower.pdf). For pattern instructions, refer to The Patterns (page 8).

Create the trapunto design and then machine stitch, quilt, and finish the piece. Refer to Shadow Trapunto Technique at a Glance (page 6); Getting Started (page 8); Shadow Trapunto Tutorial (page 12); and Machine Stitching, Quilting, and Finishing (page 16) for general information.

After washing the piece, center the 12½″-diameter transparent plastic circle template over the design. Trace around the template with a marker (it can be permanent if you are sure you placed the template correctly) and cut the quilt on the line. Add bias binding.

Day and Night

PILLOW SIZE: approximately 16½″ × 16½″ | **PATTERN SIZE:** 15″ × 15″

These two pillows are made with the same stitching design. The different results are achieved by switching the parts of the batting that are trimmed away, which reverses the positive and negative space.

Note

When making the trapunto/batting piece for the pillow design with more pink background fabric showing, be sure to stitch on the bounding square lines to create the exterior border. I recommend that you stitch these straight lines with a walking foot.

Materials and Cutting

Materials listed are for 1 pillow.

ORGANZA: 20″ × 20″

TRAPUNTO BATTING: 20″ × 20″

BACKGROUND FABRIC: 22″ × 22″

QUILT BATTING: 22″ × 22″

BACKING FABRIC: 22″ × 22″

PILLOW BACK FABRIC: 2 pieces 18½″ × 12¼″

BINDING: 1 pieced strip 2½″ × 76″

SQUARE PILLOW FORM: 16″ × 16″

Instructions

Enlarge and print the *Day and Night* pattern (page 86) or print and assemble the paper pattern using the file on the CD (dayandnight.pdf). For pattern instructions, refer to The Patterns (page 8).

Create the trapunto design and then machine stitch, quilt, and finish the piece. Refer to Shadow Trapunto Technique at a Glance (page 6); Getting Started (page 8); Shadow Trapunto Tutorial (page 12); and Machine Stitching, Quilting, and Finishing (page 16) for general information.

After washing the piece, trim the edges of the piece ¾″ from the outermost line (or points) of the design.

Hem a long side on each of the 2 pillow back pieces, assemble the pillow back, and add a hook-and-loop tape closure (see Making the Pillow Back, page 21).

Attach the pillow front to the back using Option 1 in Finishing the Pillow (page 21) and bind.

Friendship Posy

QUILT SIZE: approximately 26½″ × 26½″ | PATTERN SIZE: 20″ × 20″

Materials and Cutting

ORGANZA: 30″ × 30″

TRAPUNTO BATTING: 30″ × 30″

BACKGROUND FABRIC: 32″ × 32″

QUILT BATTING: 32″ × 32″

BACKING FABRIC: 32″ × 32″

BINDING: 1 pieced strip 2½″ × 116″

Instructions

Enlarge and print the *Friendship Posy* pattern (page 74) or print and assemble the paper pattern using the file on the CD (friendshipposy.pdf). For pattern instructions, refer to The Patterns (page 8).

Create the trapunto design and then machine stitch, quilt, and finish the piece. Refer to Shadow Trapunto Technique at a Glance (page 6); Getting Started (page 8); Shadow Trapunto Tutorial (page 12); and Machine Stitching, Quilting, and Finishing (page 116) for general information.

After washing the piece, trim the edges 3½″ from the outermost points of the design and bind.

Rhythms

QUILT SIZE: approximately 28″ × 28″ | **PATTERN SIZE:** 25″ × 25″

Materials and Cutting

ORGANZA: 31″ × 31″

TRAPUNTO BATTING: 31″ × 31″

BACKGROUND FABRIC: 33″ × 33″

QUILT BATTING: 33″ × 33″

BACKING FABRIC: 33″ × 33″

BINDING: 1 pieced strip 2½″ × 122″

Instructions

Enlarge and print the *Rhythms* pattern (page 76) or print and assemble the paper pattern using the file on the CD (rhythms.pdf). For pattern instructions, refer to The Patterns (page 8).

Create the trapunto design and then machine stitch, quilt, and finish the piece. Refer to Shadow Trapunto Technique at a Glance (page 6); Getting Started (page 8); Shadow Trapunto Tutorial (page 12); and Machine Stitching, Quilting, and Finishing (page 16) for general information.

After washing the piece, trim the edges 1½″ from the edge of the design and bind.

Happy Memories

QUILT SIZE: approximately 25½″ × 25″ | **PATTERN SIZE:** 22″ × 22″

Materials and Cutting

ORGANZA: 29″ × 28″

TRAPUNTO BATTING: 29″ × 28″

BACKGROUND FABRIC: 31″ × 30″

QUILT BATTING: 31″ × 30″

BACKING FABRIC: 31″ × 30″

BINDING: 1 pieced strip 2½″ × 111″

Instructions

Enlarge and print the *Happy Memories* pattern (page 77) or print and assemble the paper pattern using the file on the CD (happymemories.pdf). For pattern instructions, refer to The Patterns (page 8).

Create the trapunto design and then machine stitch, quilt, and finish the piece. Refer to Shadow Trapunto at a Glance (page 6); Getting Started (page 8); Shadow Trapunto Tutorial (page 12); and Machine Stitching, Quilting, and Finishing (page 16) for general information.

After washing the piece, trim the edges 2″ from the outermost points of the design and bind.

Desert Oasis

QUILT SIZE: approximately 33″ × 33″ | **PATTERN SIZE:** 30″ × 30″

Materials and Cutting

ORGANZA: 36″ × 36″

TRAPUNTO BATTING: 36″ × 36″

BACKGROUND FABRIC: 38″ × 38″

QUILT BATTING: 38″ × 38″

BACKING FABRIC: 38″ × 38″

BINDING: 1 pieced strip 2½″ × 142″

Instructions

Enlarge and print the *Desert Oasis* pattern (page 78) or print and assemble the paper pattern using the file on the CD (desertoasis.pdf). For pattern instructions, refer to The Patterns (page 8).

Create the trapunto design and then machine stitch, quilt, and finish the piece. Refer to Shadow Trapunto Technique at a Glance (page 6); Getting Started (page 8); Shadow Trapunto Tutorial (page 12); and Machine Stitching, Quilting, and Finishing (page 16) for general information.

After washing the piece, trim the edges 2″ from the outermost points of the border and bind.

Raindrops on the Lake

QUILT SIZE: approximately 26½″ × 28½″ | **PATTERN SIZE:** 25″ × 25″

Materials and Cutting

ORGANZA: 30″ × 32″

TRAPUNTO BATTING: 30″ × 32″

BACKGROUND FABRIC: 32″ × 34″

QUILT BATTING: 32″ × 34″

BACKING FABRIC: 32″ × 34″

BINDING: 1 pieced strip 2½″ × 120″

PIPING: 4 strips ⅞″ × 29″

Instructions

Enlarge and print the *Raindrops on the Lake* pattern (page 79) or print and assemble the paper pattern using the file on the CD (raindropsonthelake.pdf). For pattern instructions, refer to The Patterns (page 8).

Create the trapunto design and then machine stitch, quilt, and finish the piece. Refer to Shadow Trapunto Technique at a Glance (page 6); Getting Started (page 8); Shadow Trapunto Tutorial (page 12); and Machine Stitching, Quilting, and Finishing (page 16) for general information.

After washing the piece, trim the edges 2″ from the outermost points of the design.

To add piping, fold the strips in half lengthwise with the wrong sides together and press. Align the raw edges of the piping, right sides together, with the raw edges of the quilt top. Stitch with ⅛″ seam allowances—first on the sides and then on the top and bottom edges. Trim the ends of the piping even with the edges of the quilt. Bind the quilt, ensuring that the folded edge of the piping peeks out next to the binding.

Flower Path

QUILT SIZE: approximately 33″ × 33″ | **PATTERN SIZE:** 30″ × 30″

Materials and Cutting

ORGANZA: 36″ × 36″

TRAPUNTO BATTING: 36″ × 36″

BACKGROUND FABRIC: 38″ × 38″

QUILT BATTING: 38″ × 38″

BACKING FABRIC: 38″ × 38″

BINDING: 1 pieced strip 2½″ × 142″

Instructions

Enlarge and print the *Flower Path* pattern (page 80) or print and assemble the paper pattern using the file on the CD (flowerpath.pdf). For pattern instructions, refer to The Patterns (page 8).

Create the trapunto design and then machine stitch, quilt, and finish the piece. Refer to Shadow Trapunto Technique at a Glance (page 6); Getting Started (page 8); Shadow Trapunto Tutorial (page 12); and Machine Stitching, Quilting, and Finishing (page 16) for general information.

After washing the piece, trim the edges 2″ from the outermost points of the design and bind.

Same design. Notice how color of background fabric affects look of design.

Photo by Geta Grama

Walled Garden

QUILT SIZE: approximately 23½″ × 23½″ | **PATTERN SIZE:** 20″ × 20″

Materials and Cutting

ORGANZA: 27″ × 27″

TRAPUNTO BATTING: 27″ × 27″

BACKGROUND FABRIC: 29″ × 29″

QUILT BATTING: 29″ × 29″

BACKING FABRIC: 29″ × 29″

BINDING: 1 pieced strip 2½″ × 104″

Instructions

Enlarge and print the *Walled Garden* pattern (page 81) or print and assemble the paper pattern using the file on the CD (walledgarden.pdf). For pattern instructions, refer to The Patterns (page 8).

Create the trapunto design and then machine stitch, quilt, and finish the piece. Refer to Shadow Trapunto Technique at a Glance (page 6); Getting Started (page 8); Shadow Trapunto Tutorial (page 12); and Machine Stitching, Quilting, and Finishing (page 16) for general information.

After washing the piece, trim the edges 1¾″ from the outermost points of the border and bind.

The Coming Winter

QUILT SIZE: approximately 33″ × 32″ | **PATTERN SIZE:** 30″ × 30″

Materials and Cutting

ORGANZA: 36″ × 35″

TRAPUNTO BATTING: 36″ × 35″

BACKGROUND FABRIC: 38″ × 37″

QUILT BATTING: 38″ × 37″

BACKING FABRIC: 38″ × 37″

BINDING: 1 pieced strip 2½″ × 140″

Instructions

Enlarge and print the pattern for *The Coming Winter* (page 83) or print and assemble the paper pattern using the file on the CD (thecomingwinter.pdf). For pattern instructions, refer to The Patterns (page 8).

Create the trapunto design and then machine stitch, quilt, and finish the piece. Refer to Shadow Trapunto Technique at a Glance (page 6); Getting Started (page 8); Shadow Trapunto Tutorial (page 12); and Machine Stitching, Quilting, and Finishing (page 16) for general information.

After washing the piece, trim the edges 1¾″ from the outermost points of the design and bind.

Doily Delight

QUILT SIZE: approximately 25½″ × 25½″ | **PATTERN SIZE:** 20″ × 20″

Materials and Cutting

ORGANZA: 29″ × 29″

TRAPUNTO BATTING: 29″ × 29″

BACKGROUND FABRIC: 31″ × 31″

QUILT BATTING: 31″ × 31″

BACKING FABRIC: 31″ × 31″

BINDING: 1 pieced strip 2½″ × 112″

Instructions

Enlarge and print the *Doily Delight* pattern (page 82) or print and assemble the paper pattern using the file on the CD (doilydelight.pdf). For pattern instructions, refer to The Patterns (page 8).

Create the trapunto design and then machine stitch, quilt, and finish the piece. Refer to Shadow Trapunto Technique at a Glance (page 6); Getting Started (page 8); Shadow Trapunto Tutorial (page 12); and Machine Stitching, Quilting, and Finishing (page 16) for general information.

After washing the piece, trim the edges 3″ from the outermost points of the design and bind.

Flower and Lace

QUILT SIZE: approximately 32½″ × 32½″ | **PATTERN SIZE:** 30″ × 30″

Materials and Cutting

ORGANZA: 36″ × 36″

TRAPUNTO BATTING: 36″ × 36″

BACKGROUND FABRIC: 38″ × 38″

QUILT BATTING: 38″ × 38″

BACKING FABRIC: 38″ × 38″

BINDING: 1 pieced strip 2½″ × 140″

Instructions

Enlarge and print the *Flower and Lace* pattern (page 84) or print and assemble the paper pattern using the file on the CD (flowerandlace.pdf). For pattern instructions, refer to The Patterns (page 8).

Create the trapunto design and then machine stitch, quilt, and finish the piece. Refer to Shadow Trapunto Technique at a Glance (page 6); Getting Started (page 8); Shadow Trapunto Tutorial (page 12); and Machine Stitching, Quilting, and Finishing (page 16) for general information.

Pin very well before stitching the pattern. After washing the piece, trim the edges 1¾″ from the outermost points of the design and bind.

Highland Paths

QUILT SIZE: approximately 34″ × 34″ | **PATTERN SIZE:** 30″ × 30″

Materials and Cutting

ORGANZA: 37″ × 37″

TRAPUNTO BATTING: 37″ × 37″

BACKGROUND FABRIC: 39″ × 39″

QUILT BATTING: 39″ × 39″

BACKING FABRIC: 39″ × 39″

BINDING: 1 pieced strip 2½″ × 146″

Instructions

Enlarge and print the *Highland Paths* pattern (page 85) or print and assemble the paper pattern using the file on the CD (highlandpaths.pdf). For pattern instructions, refer to The Patterns (page 8).

Create the trapunto design and then machine stitch, quilt, and finish the piece. Refer to Shadow Trapunto Technique at a Glance (page 6); Getting Started (page 8); Shadow Trapunto Tutorial (page 12); and Machine Stitching, Quilting, and Finishing (page 16) for general information.

After washing the piece, trim the edges 2″ from the outermost points of the design and bind.

Edelweiss

QUILT SIZE: approximately 18½″ × 18½″ | **PATTERN SIZE:** 14″ × 14″

Materials and Cutting

ORGANZA: 22″ × 22″

TRAPUNTO BATTING: 22″ × 22″

GREEN: 24″ × 24″ for background and 12 squares 3″ × 3″ for prairie points

QUILT BATTING: 24″ × 24″

BACKING FABRIC: 24″ × 24″

RED: 12 squares 3″ × 3″ for prairie points and 1 pieced strip 2½″ × 84″ for binding

Instructions

Enlarge and print the *Edelweiss* pattern (page 77) or print and assemble the paper pattern using the file on the CD (edelweiss.pdf). For pattern instructions, refer to The Patterns (page 8).

Create the trapunto design and then machine stitch, quilt, and finish the piece. Refer to Shadow Trapunto Technique at a Glance (page 6); Getting Started (page 8); Shadow Trapunto Tutorial (page 12); and Machine Stitching, Quilting, and Finishing (page 16) for general information.

After washing the piece, trim the edges 2½″ from the outermost points of the design.

Lay the red and green squares (wrong sides up) on your pressing surface. Fold the squares in half diagonally and press. Fold in half diagonally again and press.

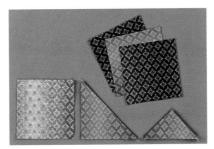

Prairie points

Baste the prairie points to the edges of the quilt, aligning the raw edges of the prairie points with the raw edges of the quilt, spacing them evenly (refer to the photo for placement), and using ⅛″ seam allowances. Bind.

Daisy Postcard

POSTCARD SIZE: 4″ × 6″ | **PATTERN SIZE:** 3″ × 4″

Materials and Cutting

ORGANZA: 6″ × 8″

TRAPUNTO BATTING: 4″ × 6″

BACKGROUND FABRIC FOR TOP: 6″ × 8″

QUILT BATTING: 6″ × 8″

BACKING FABRIC: 6″ × 8″

CARDBOARD: 4″ × 6″

TRANSPARENT PLASTIC TEMPLATE: 4″ × 6″

GLUE

PERMANENT MARKER

Instructions

Print the *Daisy Postcard* pattern (page 73) or print the paper pattern using the file on the CD (daisypostcard.pdf). For pattern instructions, refer to The Patterns (page 8).

Create the trapunto design and then machine stitch, quilt, and finish the piece. Refer to Shadow Trapunto Technique at a Glance (page 6); Getting Started (page 8); Shadow Trapunto Tutorial (page 12); and Machine Stitching, Quilting, and Finishing (page 16) for general information.

Quilt the background with stippling or try different filler designs.

After washing the piece, place the 4″ × 6″ plastic template on top of the postcard. Move it around on the flower until you are happy with the position of the flower. Trace around the template with a marker (it can be permanent if you are sure you placed the template correctly) and cut the postcard on the line.

Apply permanent glue onto the edges, in the center, and in a few other places on the back of the 4″ × 6″ cardboard. Then put the quilted piece on top of it and apply pressure with your fingers. Don't stretch the quilted piece!

Finish the edges using a machine zigzag stitch, satin stitch, or blanket stitch. When stitching through all the layers (including the cardboard), be careful that you don't make your stitching too dense or the cardboard might tear. Make a test first.

Notes

Try these variations as well:

- Enlarge the pattern to make larger cards.

- Combine shadow trapunto with appliqués or patchwork.

- Make a monogram postcard using your favorite font instead of the flower.

Monogram Portfolio

PORTFOLIO SIZE: approximately 14¼″ × 12¼″ | **PATTERN SIZE:** 10″ × 10″

Materials and Cutting

ORGANZA: 2 pieces 18″ × 16″

TRAPUNTO BATTING: 18″ × 16″

TOP FABRIC: 2 pieces 18″ × 16″

BACKING FABRIC: 2 pieces 18″ × 16″

FAST2FUSE HEAVYWEIGHT FUSIBLE INTERFACING: 2 pieces 18″ × 16″

LINING: 2 pieces 18″ × 16″

BINDING: 1 strip 2½″ × 40″

HANDLES: 2 strips 3″ × 13″

JEANS/DENIM NEEDLE: Size #16/100

TEMPORARY ADHESIVE SPRAY (*optional*)

BUTTONS: 2, 1″ diameter

Instructions

Enlarge and print the *Monogram Portfolio* pattern (page 86) or print and assemble the paper pattern using the file on the CD (monogramportfolio.pdf). For pattern instructions, refer to The Patterns (page 8).

Monograms are not included on the CD; choose the monogram letter in a computer font you like and enlarge it to approximately 4¾″ high. Print and trace it onto the pattern.

Create the trapunto design. Refer to Shadow Trapunto Technique at a Glance (page 6), Getting Started (page 8), and Shadow Trapunto Tutorial (page 12).

To make the portfolio front, stitch and cut away the trapunto design.

Fuse a piece of top fabric on one side of the fusible interfacing and a piece of backing fabric on the other side. Position the trapunto on the top fabric and pin.

TIP

If you find it difficult to pin, use a temporary adhesive spray to glue the organza onto the top fabric.

Refer to Machine Stitching, Quilting, and Finishing (page 16) for general information.

Quilt through all the layers and wash the quilted piece. Cut the piece 3″ away from the outermost line of the trapunto design on the sides and 1¾″ away from the outermost line of the design on the top and bottom. The piece should measure about 15¼″ (width) × 12¾″ (length).

To make the portfolio back, follow the instructions for making the portfolio front, except use a plain piece of organza instead of a trapunto design piece. Trim the portfolio back to match the portfolio front piece.

Stack the 2 lining pieces on top of each other, place the portfolio back on top, trace around it, and trim both lining pieces on the line.

Fold and press the strips for handles in half lengthwise, wrong sides together. Open and press the long edges to the center fold. Refold in half and press. Topstitch along the edges. Be sure the handles are the same length; trim if necessary.

Place the front and back of the portfolio right sides together and pin. Stitch the long bottom edges and the shorter sides using a ½″ seam allowance. Stitch a second time over the first seamline for durability.

Press the seam allowances open. Clip the corners and turn the piece right side out.

Follow the same process as with the front and back with the 2 pieces of lining, except keep the lining wrong side out.

Pin the ends of a handle on the top edge of the portfolio front, aligning the raw edges. Place one end 5″ from the left side edge and the other end 5″ from the right side edge. Sew ⅛″ away from the top edge. Attach the other handle in the same way to the portfolio back.

Slip the lining (wrong side out) into the portfolio (right side out), aligning the raw edges. Match the side seams and pin. Stitch ⅛″ from the top edges, joining the portfolio and the lining.

Finish the edges with binding (see Finishing, page 19) in the same way you bind a quilt.

Turn the handles up and sew buttons through the handle on the portfolio front.

Cranberry Pie

PILLOW SIZE: approximately 15½″ diameter including ruffle | **PATTERN SIZE:** 12″ × 12″

The ruffle adds a soft touch to the edge of this pillow. For a more interesting look I made the ruffle out of two fabrics.

Materials and Cutting

ORGANZA: 17″ × 17″

TRAPUNTO BATTING: 17″ × 17″

BACKGROUND FABRIC: 19″ × 19″

QUILT BATTING: 19″ × 19″

BACKING FABRIC: 19″ × 19″

PILLOW BACK FABRIC: 2 pieces 16½″ × 11¼″

RUFFLE FABRIC 1: 1 pieced strip 1″ × 90″

RUFFLE FABRIC 2: 1 pieced strip 1″ × 90″ and 1 strip 2″ × 90″

ROUND PILLOW FORM: 14″ diameter

TRANSPARENT PLASTIC TEMPLATE: 14½″ diameter

Instructions

Enlarge and print the *Cranberry Pie* pattern (page 86) or print and assemble the paper pattern using the file on the CD (cranberrypie.pdf). For pattern instructions, refer to The Patterns (page 8).

Create the trapunto design and then machine stitch, quilt, and finish the piece. Refer to Shadow Trapunto Technique at a Glance (page 6); Getting Started (page 8); Shadow Trapunto Tutorial (page 12); and Machine Stitching, Quilting, and Finishing (page 16) for general information.

After washing the piece, make a 14½"-diameter transparent plastic circle template, center it over the design, trace around the template with a marker (it can be permanent if you are sure you placed the template correctly), and cut on the line.

Piece the 3 strips for the ruffle, with the ruffle fabric 1 (lavender) strip in the center. Press the pieced strips in half lengthwise with the wrong sides together. Set your machine to the longest stitch setting and loosen the top thread tension a bit. Baste ⅛" from the raw edges, leaving the thread tails long. Gently pull the bottom thread to gather the ruffle so it fits the edge of the pillow top (it should measure about 45" long).

Make the Pillow Back

Hem a long side on each of the 2 pieces, assemble the pillow back, and add a hook-and-loop tape closure (see Making the Pillow Back, page 21).

Attach the pillow front to the back, right sides together, using a ½" seam allowance. Trim the back even with the front and turn the pillow cover right side out and insert the pillow form.

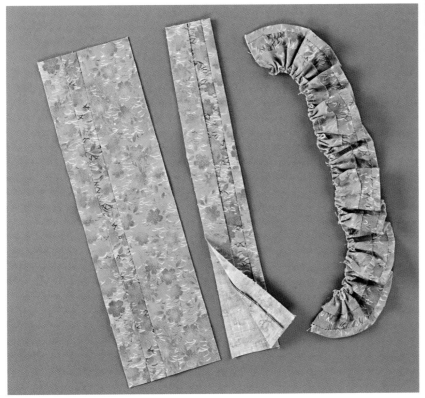

Make ruffle.

Line up the raw edge of the ruffle with the edge of the pillow and pin, adjusting the gathers evenly. Baste ¼" from the edge.

Nine-Patch Revival

QUILT SIZE: approximately 18″ × 18″ | **PATTERN SIZE:** 16″ × 16″

It is easy to add more color to quilts and enhance their design by combining shadow trapunto with appliqués. The technique is very simple: the appliqués are added to the background fabric, and then the organza / batting trapunto piece is layered on top of them.

Materials and Cutting

ORGANZA: 21″ × 21″

TRAPUNTO BATTING: 21″ × 21″

BACKGROUND FABRIC: 23″ × 23″

ACCENT FABRICS: 5 squares 3½″ × 3½″ and 4 squares 3″ × 3″ (use 1–9 fabrics)

QUILT BATTING: 23″ × 23″

BACKING FABRIC: 23″ × 23″

BINDING: 1 pieced strip 2½″ × 82″

FABRIC GLUE: Any kind of glue, permanent or temporary; just be sure it will not show on the fabric after washing.

Instructions

Enlarge and print the *Nine-Patch Revival* pattern (page 82) or print and assemble the paper pattern using the file on the CD (ninepatchrevival.pdf). For pattern instructions, refer to The Patterns (page 8).

Tape the paper pattern onto a window and add the background fabric on top of it. Using the pattern (the 9 squares drawn with thick lines) as a reference, glue the accent squares onto the background.

Position accent squares on background fabric.

Create the trapunto design and then machine stitch, quilt, and finish the piece. Refer to Shadow Trapunto Technique at a Glance (page 6); Getting Started (page 8); Shadow Trapunto Tutorial (page 12); and Machine Stitching, Quilting, and Finishing (page 16) for general information.

After washing the piece, trim the edges 1″ from the outermost points of the border and bind.

Notes

- It is not necessary to sew the edges of the appliqué pieces to the background, but if you prefer to sew the appliqués in place, you can use invisible or water-soluble thread.

- Do not start stitching the design before placing the appliqués on the background fabric; if you do, you will need a new pattern as a guide for appliqué placement.

- When stitching the design, be careful not to stitch on the thick lines drawn for the placement of the appliqués.

Christmas Romance

QUILT SIZE: approximately 19½″ × 19½″ | **PATTERN SIZE:** 16″ × 16″ (Method 1) or 8″ × 8″ (Methods 2 and 3)

TIP

Use fabrics in different colors but with a similar value. Do not mix light and dark colors, because they affect the trapunto design in different ways. The combination of dark red and dark green is better than dark red and light green.

Combining shadow trapunto with patchwork is another way of making a colorful shadow trapunto quilt. The quilt will not be a wholecloth quilt, as the background fabric is pieced. You can make a pieced shadow trapunto quilt using any of the following three methods.

METHOD 1:

Add wholecloth trapunto organza to a pieced background.

This method requires accurate piecing and works great for small quilts with only a few blocks.

Materials and Cutting

ORGANZA: 23″ × 23″

TRAPUNTO BATTING: 23″ × 23″

RED: 2 squares 8½″ × 8½″, 2 strips 2″ × 16½″, and 2 strips 2″ × 19½″ for borders

GREEN: 2 squares 8½″ × 8½″

QUILT BATTING: 25″ × 25″

BACKING FABRIC: 25″ × 25″

BINDING: 1 pieced strip 2½″ × 88″

Instructions

Enlarge and print the *Christmas Romance* pattern (page 74) or print and assemble the paper pattern using the file on the CD (christmasromance.pdf). For pattern instructions, refer to The Patterns (page 8).

Note that this pattern has 4 repeats of the single block design.

Create the trapunto design. Refer to Shadow Trapunto Technique at a Glance (page 6); Getting Started (page 8); Shadow Trapunto Tutorial (page 12); and Machine Stitching, Quilting, and Finishing (page 16) for general information.

Stitch and cut away the trapunto design.

Using a ¼″ seam allowance, piece the red and green squares, and then add the red borders. Press. Center the trapunto on the pieced background.

Piece background; add borders.

Wholecloth trapunto organza layered on pieced background

Add the batting and backing and then finish stitch the design motifs. Quilt, wash, and bind.

METHOD 2:

Make individual background fabric / trapunto organza blocks and then assemble the blocks.

This method works great for large quilts. It creates bulky seam allowances, but the final quilting will flatten the seams.

Individual block

Materials and Cutting

ORGANZA: 4 squares 10″ × 10″

TRAPUNTO BATTING:
4 squares 10″ × 10″

RED: 2 squares 8½″ × 8½″,
2 strips 2″ × 16½″, and
2 strips 2″ × 19½″ for borders

GREEN: 2 squares 8½″ × 8½″

Instructions

Enlarge and print the *Christmas Romance* block pattern (page 75) or print and assemble the paper pattern using the file on the CD (christmasromanceblock.pdf) 4 times to make 4 blocks. For pattern instructions, refer to The Patterns (page 8).

Create the trapunto design. Refer to Shadow Trapunto Technique at a Glance (page 6); Getting Started (page 8); Shadow Trapunto Tutorial (page 12); and Machine Stitching, Quilting, and Finishing (page 16) for general information.

Using the organza squares, trapunto batting, and 4 paper patterns, stitch the designs. Cut the batting away and trim the organza/batting pieces to 8½″ × 8½″, being careful to keep the design in the center of the trimmed squares. Baste the organza/batting piece onto a background square approximately ⅛″ from the edges of the block by hand or by machine. Repeat to make 4 blocks. Assemble the blocks using ¼″ seam allowances. Add the borders and press to make the front of the quilt. Note that with Method 2, the borders do not have a layer of organza on top.

Notes

- Press the seams only on the back and *do not use steam.*

- On the front, finger-press the seams. If you have a narrow iron you can press on the front too, but be careful not to press the batting.

Individual blocks assembled

Add batting and backing and quilt as desired. Wash the piece and bind. (I did not trim the border after washing.)

METHOD 3:

Make individual background fabric / trapunto organza blocks, quilt, and then assemble the blocks.

If you prefer to work on a small scale, a big quilt can be sewn and quilted in sections.

Use the pattern and instructions for Method 2, except quilt each block before assembling the blocks into the quilt, using your favorite quilt-as-you-go method.

Quilted block

Octagonal Kaleidoscope

QUILT SIZE: approximately 15½″ × 15½″ | **PATTERN SIZE:** 15″ × 15″

Materials and Cutting

TRIANGLES: 8 triangles fussy cut from 8½″-wide strips (Make a template from the octagon triangle pattern, page 56.)
Note: I always cut the strips parallel to the selvage and place the base of the triangle template on the edge of a strip.

ORGANZA: 19″ × 19

TRAPUNTO BATTING: 19″ × 19″

QUILT BATTING: 21″ × 21″

BACKING: 21″ × 21″

BINDING: 1 pieced strip 2½″ × 62″

Instructions

Enlarge and print the *Octagonal Kaleidoscope* pattern (page 81) or print the paper pattern using the file on the CD (octagonalkaleidoscope.pdf). For pattern instructions, refer to The Patterns (page 8).

Using a ¼″ seam allowance, piece the triangles to make the octagon background. Press.

Create the trapunto design and then machine stitch, quilt, and finish the piece. Refer to Shadow Trapunto Technique at a Glance (page 6); Getting Started (page 8); Shadow Trapunto Tutorial (page 12); and Machine Stitching, Quilting, and Finishing (page 16) for general information.

After washing the piece, trim the edges 1″ from the outermost points of the design wedges (see Quilts with More than Four Sides, page 18) and bind.

8 triangles with identical print placement

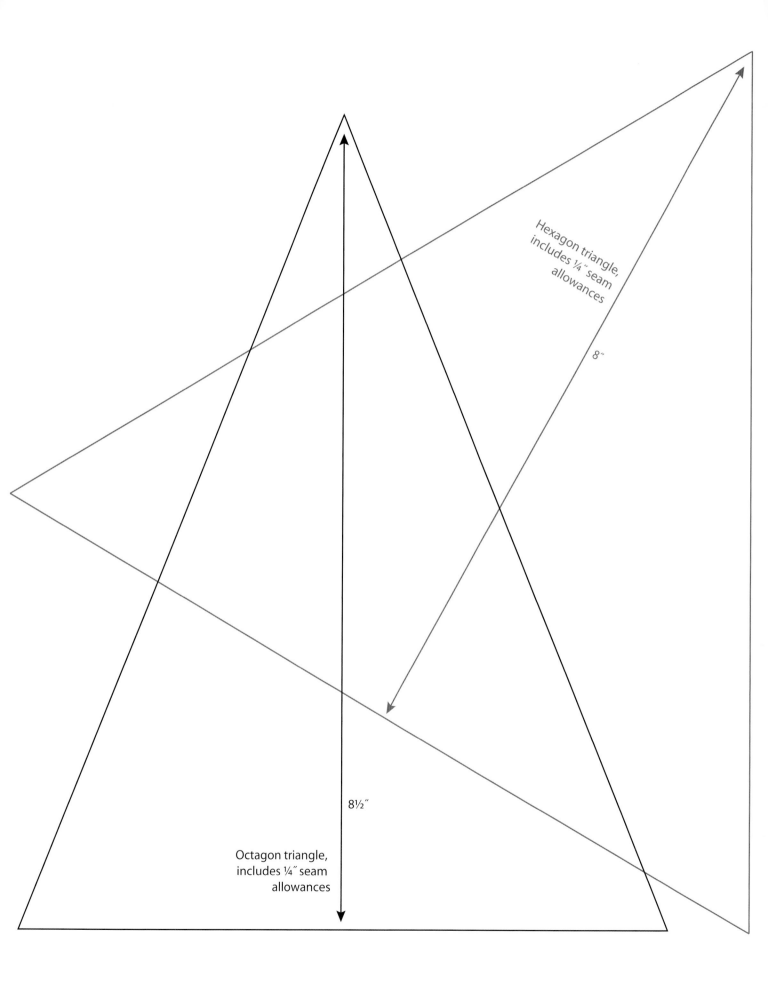

Hexagon triangle, includes ¼˝ seam allowances

8˝

8½˝

Octagon triangle, includes ¼˝ seam allowances

Hexagonal Kaleidoscope

QUILT SIZE: approximately 17½″ × 15″ | **PATTERN SIZE:** 15″ × 15″

Materials and Cutting

TRIANGLES: 6 equilateral triangles fussy cut from 8″-wide strips (Make a template from the hexagon triangle pattern, page 56.) *Note: I always cut the strips parallel to the selvage and place the base of the triangle template on the edge of a strip.*

ORGANZA: 21″ × 18″

TRAPUNTO BATTING: 21″ × 18″

QUILT BATTING: 23″ × 20″

BACKING: 23″ × 20″

BINDING: 1 pieced strip 2½″ × 60″

Instructions

Enlarge and print the *Hexagonal Kaleidoscope* pattern (page 81) or print and assemble the paper pattern using the file on the CD (hexagonalkaleidoscope.pdf). For pattern instructions, refer to The Patterns (page 8).

Using a ¼″ seam allowance, piece the triangles to make the hexagon. Press.

Create the trapunto design and then machine stitch, quilt, and finish the piece. Refer to Shadow Trapunto Technique at a Glance (page 6); Getting Started (page 8); Shadow Trapunto Tutorial (page 12); and Machine Stitching, Quilting, and Finishing (page 16) for general information.

After washing the piece, trim the edges 1″ from the outermost points of the design wedges (see Quilts with More than Four Sides, page 18) and bind.

6 equilateral triangles with identical print

SNOWFLAKES, 2007, 40" × 40"
MINI-SNOWFLAKES, 2007, 15" × 15"

These two quilts were among my first shadow trapunto quilts. After I made the large quilt I tried a smaller one. Making smaller shadow trapunto quilts has its advantages and disadvantages. Though less time is needed for stitching and quilting, extra precision is required. Depending on the size of the miniature and the complexity of the designs, cutting the batting away might be a longer process. I learned that for small work it is necessary to use water-soluble thread in the bobbin too.

OLD-FASHIONED TREAT, 2008, 39¾″ × 39½″

I love the lacy look of this quilt. Quilting with different threads in the interior and exterior
of the wreath changes the color of this wonderful quilt; the quilting must be very dense.

SUMMER RAIN, 2008, 38½″ × 38½″

The first thing you notice in this quilt is the high contrast between the white of the trapunto design and the background fabric.

PASSIONS, 2008, 52½" × 52¾"

I think the name of this quilt is well deserved. I worked two months on it. I spent two weeks (and many hours a day) only cutting the batting away. Some motifs are very small. The smallest circles in the wreaths are ⅛".

DANCING FEATHERS, 2008, 37½″ × 38½″

I chose a lighter background color than I usually use under organza. I love the subtle, smooth transition between the batting and background. This quilt is entirely stitched with invisible thread and has a beautiful texture. The back is as beautiful as the front.

Detail of Dancing Feathers

Back of Dancing Feathers

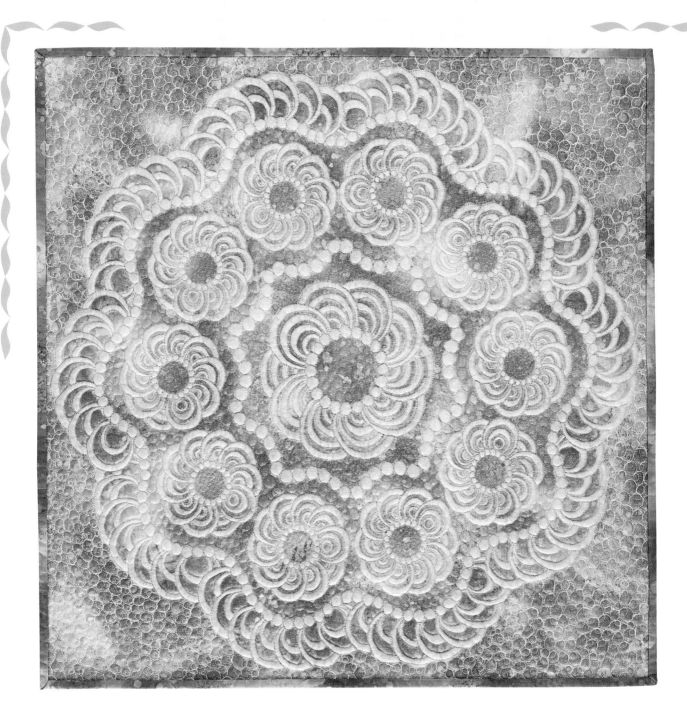

WHITE BOUQUET, 2008, 19½″ × 19½″

This small quilt is one of the quilts I love most. I really wanted to make it smaller, but it would have been almost impossible to cut away the batting between the smallest motifs. The smallest space between the petals of the flowers is ¹⁄₁₆″, and the smallest circle is a little larger than ⅛″.

DANCING FLOWERS, 2008, 19½″ × 19½″

This is a small, very detailed quilt. There was a lot of intricate cutting, but it was worth it.

Photo by Geta Grama

POINSETTIA, 2009, 14¾″ × 14¾″

Here I gave definition to a simple trapunto design with colored threads. This method has a lot of potential for future experimentation.

BOWL, 2010, 13″ top diameter

I started this bowl like any other quilt, but instead of the middle batting I used a piece of fast2fuse, a heavyweight fusible interfacing (see Resources, page 87). I fused the top and back fabric to the interfacing and then added the trapunto design stitched on organza. I quilted through all the layers and then shaped the bowl. The heavyweight interfacing gives a very stiff and firm look to a bowl.

Photo by Geta Grama

MERCI MYLENE! 2009, 14″ × 21″

This quilt is one of the most exciting projects I have ever made. While I quilt, I usually listen to music, and Mylene Farmer is my favorite singer. She is one of the most successful artists of all time in France. I saw her in Paris performing in three concerts. Those days were the most beautiful days of my life. I wanted to thank her for the wonderful music I listen to every day, so I made this quilt for her.

Lettering with batting is incredibly easy. You don't even need a pattern. Just take a piece of paper, write a message by hand for someone you love, and quilt it. Put your message on a pillow, a small wallhanging, a book cover, a bag, or even a card.

Patterns

© 2012 Geta Grama

Foliage Tutorial (page 12)
Enlarge 400% to 15″ × 15″.

© 2012 Geta Grama

A New Beginning (page 26)
Enlarge 400% to 15″ × 15″.

© 2012 Geta Grama

Batting Test (page 10)
Enlarge 200% to 6″ × 6″.

© 2012 Geta Grama

Lacy Flower (page 30)
Enlarge 200% to 8″ × 8″.

© 2012 Geta Grama

Waves (page 22)
Enlarge 400% to 25″ × 25″.

Indian Summer (page 23)
Enlarge 400% to 20″ × 20″.

© 2012 Geta Grama

Round Dance of Christmas Trees
(page 24)
Enlarge 400% to 12″ × 12″.

© 2012 Geta Grama

Fortune Wheel (page 25)
Enlarge 400% to 16″ × 16″.

© 2012 Geta Grama

Waiting for Spring (page 27)
Enlarge 400% to 20″ × 40″.

Daisy Postcard (page 44)
Pattern sized at 100%.

© 2012 Geta Grama

Lights into the Dark (page 28)
Enlarge 400% to 16½" × 38".

© 2012 Geta Grama

Christmas Romance (page 52)
Enlarge 400% to 16″ × 16″.

© 2012 Geta Grama

Friendship Posy (page 32)
Enlarge 400% to 20″ × 20″.

© 2012 Geta Grama

Christmas Romance block (page 52)
Enlarge 200% to 8″ × 8″.

© 2012 Geta Grama

Polar Night (page 29)
Enlarge 400% to 20″ × 20″.

© 2012 Geta Grama

Rhythms (page 33)
Enlarge 400% to 25″ × 25″.

Edelweiss (page 43)
Enlarge 400% to 14″ × 14″.

© 2012 Geta Grama

Happy Memories (page 34)
Enlarge 400% to 22″ × 22″.

© 2012 Geta Grama

Desert Oasis (page 35)
Enlarge 400% to 30″ × 30″.

© 2012 Geta Grama

Raindrops on the Lake (page 36)
Enlarge 400% to 25″ × 25″.

Flower Path (page 37)
Enlarge 400% to 30″ × 30″.

Walled Garden (page 38)
Enlarge 400% to 20″ × 20″.

© 2012 Geta Grama

Hexagonal Kaleidoscope (page 57)
Enlarge 400% to 15″ × 15″.

© 2012 Geta Grama

Octagonal Kaleidoscope (page 55)
Enlarge 400% to 15″ × 15″.

© 2012 Geta Grama

Nine-Patch Revival (page 50)
Enlarge 400% to 16″ × 16″.

© 2012 Geta Grama

Doily Delight (page 40)
Enlarge 400% to 20″ × 20″.

© 2012 Geta Grama

The Coming Winter (page 39)
Enlarge 400% to 30″ × 30″.

Flower and Lace (page 41)
Enlarge 400% to 30″ × 30″.

© 2012 Geta Grama

Highland Paths (page 42)
Enlarge 400% to 30″ × 30″.

Monogram Portfolio (page 46)
Enlarge 200% to 10″ × 10″.

© 2012 Geta Grama

Cranberry Pie (page 48)
Enlarge 400% to 12″ × 12″.

© 2012 Geta Grama

Day and Night (page 31)
Enlarge 400% to 15″ × 15″.

© 2012 Geta Grama

About the Author

Geta Grama's crafting journey started in 2000, when she discovered quilting, absolutely by chance, on the Internet. Seduced by the new world of combining fabrics, colors, and patterns, she abandoned her engineering profession and all other passions and devoted her time entirely to quilting. She lives in Romania with her husband, Mircea, who always encourages her to follow her passion. Her family members are her biggest fans.

Though it is not easy to quilt in a country where the word *quilt* is unknown to most people, she could not imagine her life without quilting. For her free tutorials and quilting ideas, visit her website (www.RomanianQuiltStudio.com) and her blog (cadouri-din-inima.blogspot.com).

Resources

ORGANZA   www.papermart.com

**ORGANZA, BATTING, THREAD SNIPS,
SEWING MACHINE NEEDLES**   www.joann.com

WATER-SOLUBLE THREAD, TOPSTITCH NEEDLES
www.jhittlesewing.funoverload.com/sewing/catalog.php

BATTING   www.fairfieldworld.com
www.hobbsbondedfibers.com
www.batt-mart.com

**FAST2FUSE HEAVYWEIGHT INTERFACING,
CAROL DOAK'S FOUNDATION PAPER**
www.ctpub.com

**BATTING, THREAD SNIPS, WATER-SOLUBLE THREAD,
SEWING MACHINE NEEDLES**
www.asding.com (UK supplier)

Great Titles *from* C&T PUBLISHING

Available at your local retailer or **www.ctpub.com** *or* **800-284-1114**

For a list of other fine books from C&T Publishing, visit our website to view our catalog online.

C&T PUBLISHING, INC.

P.O. Box 1456
Lafayette, CA 94549
800-284-1114

Email: ctinfo@ctpub.com
Website: www.ctpub.com

C&T Publishing's professional photography services are now available to the public. Visit us at www.ctmediaservices.com.

Tips and Techniques can be found at www.ctpub.com > Consumer Resources > Quiltmaking Basics: Tips & Techniques for Quiltmaking & More

For quilting supplies:

COTTON PATCH

1025 Brown Ave.
Lafayette, CA 94549
Store: 925-284-1177
Mail order: 925-283-7883

Email: CottonPa@aol.com
Website: www.quiltusa.com

Note: Fabrics used in the quilts shown may not be currently available, as fabric manufacturers keep most fabrics in print for only a short time.